CONCISE COLLECTION

Top Gun Aircraft

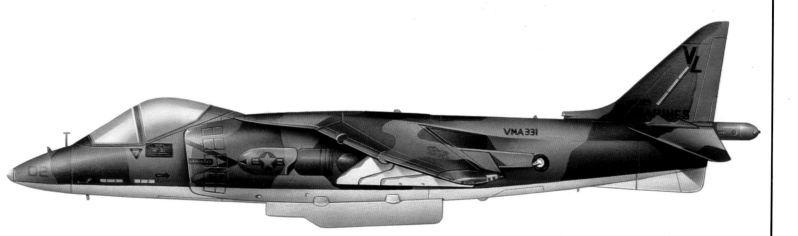

Christopher Chant

Grange
BOOKS

Published in 1995
by Grange Books
An imprint of Grange Books Plc.
The Grange
Grange Yard
London SE1 3AG

ISBN 1 85627 787 9

Printed in Italy.

Acknowledgments
All photographs supplied by BTPH with the
assistance of the following companies:
Aermacchi, Atlas Aircraft, British Aerospace
Industries, Casa, Dassault-Breguet, Embraer,
Israel Aircraft Industries, McDonnell Douglas,
Northrop, Saab-Scania, US Department of
Defense, with the exception of Aviation
Photographs International/Jeremy Flack 36;
Nikk Burridge 14; Czechoslovak Embassy 3:
Quadrant Picture Library 24, 26, 27, 37, 39.

All artworks supplied by Maltings Partnership
except: Andrew Wright 24.

Contents

Aeritalia/Aermacchi/Embraer AMX	6
Aermacchi MB. 339K Veltro 2	7
Aero L-39ZA Albatros	8
Atlas Aircraft Corporation Cheetah D	9
British Aerospace Hawk 200	10
British Aerospace Sea Harrier FRS.Mk 1	11
Casa C-101CC Aviojet	12
Dassault-Breguet Mirage 50	13
Dassault-Breguet Mirage 2000DA	14
Dassault-Breguet Mirage F1C	15
Dassault-Breguet Rafale-A	16
Dassault-Breguet Super Etendard	17
Dassault-Breguet/Dornier Alpha Jet 1	18
Eurofighter EFA	19
Fairchild Republic A-10A Thunderbolt II	20
General Dynamics F-16C Fighting Falcon	21
Grumman F-14A Tomcat	22
Israel Aircraft Industries Kfir-C7	23
Lockheed F-117A	24
McDonnell Douglas F-15C Eagle	25
McDonnell Douglas F/A-18C Hornet	26
McDonnell Douglas/British Aerospace AV-8B Harrier II	27
McDonnell Douglas/Israel Aircraft Industries Phantom 2000	28
Mikoyan-Gurevich MiG-21BIS 'Fishbed-L'	29
Mikoyan-Gurevich MiG-23MG 'Flogger-G'	30
Mikoyan-Gurevich MiG-25M 'Foxbat-E'	31
Mikoyan-Gurevich MiG-27 'Flogger-D'	32
Mikoyan-Gurevich MiG-29 'Fulcrum-A'	33
Mitsubishi F1	34
Northrop F-5E Tiger II	35
Panavia Tornado ADV	36
Saab-Scania JA 37 Viggen	37
Saab-Scania JAS 39 Gripen	38
Sepecat Jaguar GR.Mk1	39
Shenyang J-6C 'Farmer'	40
Shenyang J-8-1 'Finback'	41
Singapore Aircraft Industries A-4 Super Skyhawk	42
Sukhoi Su-7BMK 'Fitter-A'	43
Sukhoi Su-24 'Fencer-C'	44
Sukhoi Su-27 'Flanker-B'	45
Yakovlev Yak-38 'Forger-A'	46
Glossary	

Left: On the deck of the USS Constellation, *an F/A-18 Hornet is prepared for catapult launch.*

Aeritalia/Aermacchi/ Embraer AMX

Entering service from 1988, the AMX was designed as a 'no frills' attack fighter of modest size and electronic simplicity to keep down costs without undue sacrifice of capabilities: the result is a transonic type without radar, but with otherwise capable electronics.

The type has been produced in single- and two-seat AMX(T) variants, the Brazilian version differing mainly in having two 30mm cannon. A later anti-ship model will have radar and specialist missiles.

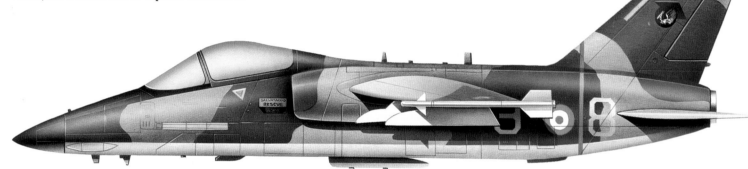

Countries of Origin: Italy and Brazil
Type: single-seat light ground attack, close air support and reconnaissance fighter
Crew: one
Power Plant: one Piaggio-built Rolls-Royce Spey Mk 807 non-afterburning turbofan, rated at 49.1kN (11,023 lb) thrust
Dimensions: span 8.874m (29 ft 1.4 in); length 13.575m (44 ft 6.5 in); height 4.58m (15 ft 0.2 in); wing area 21.00m² (226.04 sq ft)
Weights: empty 6,000kg (13,228 lb); loaded 12,500 kg (27,557 lb)
Performance: maximum speed 1,163km/h (723 mph); service ceiling 13,000m (42,650 ft); range 370km (230 miles) radius with a 2,722kg (6,000 lb) warload
Armament: one 20mm M61A1 Vulcan cannon and provision for up to 3,800kg (7,377 lb) of disposable stores

An AMX prototype carrying Sidewinder missiles at the wingtips.

Aermacchi MB.339K Veltro 2

This is the dedicated ground attack variant on the MB.339 basic trainer with the rear-cockpit volume used for fuel and avionics. The type first flew in May 1980, and though performance is not superior to that of the trainer, operational capability is much enhanced by features such as a digital inertial navigation and attack system (with a laser rangefinder) data being fed to the pilot via a head-up display and head-down displays.

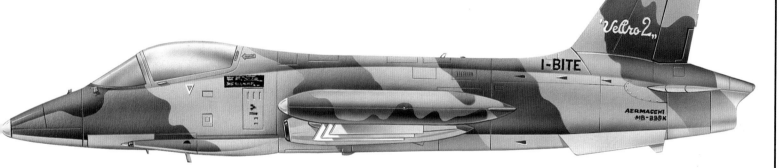

Country of Origin: Italy
Type: light ground attack and operational trainer
Crew: one
Power Plant: one Piaggio-built Rolls-Royce Viper Mk 632-43 non-afterburning turbojet, rated at 19.57kN (4,400 lb) thrust
Dimensions: span 10.858m (35 ft 7.5 in) over standard tiptanks or 11.045m (35 ft 2.75 in) over circular tiptanks; length 10.792m (35 ft 5 in); height 3.90m (12 ft 9.5 in); wing area 19.30m² (207.74 sq ft)
Weights: empty 3,175kg (7,000 lb); loaded 6,150kg (13,558 lb)
Performance: maximum speed 900km/h (559 mph); service ceiling 13,565m (44,500 ft); range 376km (234 miles) radius with a 1,088kg (2,400 lb) warload
Armament: two 30mm cannon plus provision for up to 1,815kg (4,001 lb) of disposable stores

An Aermacchi MB-339K company demonstration aircraft.

Aero L-39ZA Albatros

The L-39C first flew in November 1968 and is the Warsaw Pact's standard for basic and advanced training. The L-39ZO is the weapon training variant, and from this was developed the L-39ZA dedicated light attack variant. In 1987 Aero flew the first upgraded L-39MS with a modernized cockpit and a 21.57kN (4,850 lb) thrust turbofan for better training performance, and an attack model with this engine can be expected in due course.

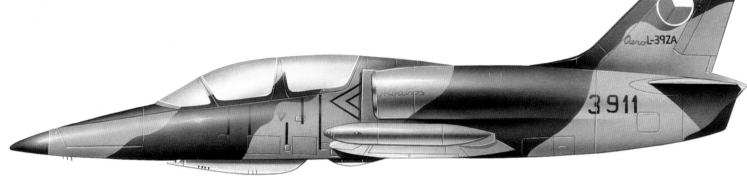

Country of Origin: Czechoslovakia
Type: light ground attack fighter
Crew: two
Power Plant: one Walter Titan (Ivchyenko AI-25-TL) non-afterburning turbofan, rated at 16.87kN (3,792 lb) thrust
Dimensions: span 9.46m (31 ft 0.5 in); length 12.32m (40 ft 5 in); height 4.72m (15ft 5.5 in); wing area 18.80m² (202.36 sq ft)
Weights: empty 3,330kg (7,341 lb); loaded 5,270kg (11,618 lb)
Performance: maximum speed 630km/h (390 mph); service ceiling 9,000m (29,530 ft); range 780km (485 miles)
Armament: one 23mm GSh-23L twin-barrel cannon plus provision for up to 1,100kg (2,425 lb) of disposable stores

An Albatros trainer aircraft, its large cockpit canopy giving both the instructor and pupil a good field of view.

Atlas Aircraft Corporation Cheetah D

In July 1987 the South African Air Force declared operational its first Cheetah fighters. The type is a radical reconstruction of Mirage IIIs along the lines pioneered by the Israelis with their Kfir development, though retaining the original SNECMA engine. The Cheetah D is the single-seat conversion of the Mirage IIICZ and IIIEZ, while the Cheetah E is the radar-carrying and thus combat-capable conversion of the two-seat Mirage IIIBZ and IIIDZ.

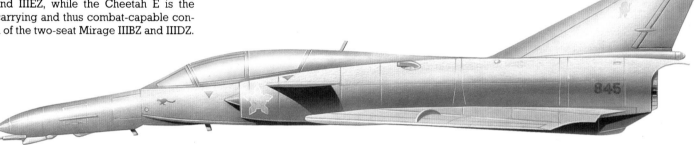

Country of Origin: South Africa
Type: multi-role fighter
Crew: one
Power Plant: one SNECMA Atar 9K-50 afterburning turbojet, rated at 70.6kN (15,873 lb) thrust
Dimensions: span 8.22m (26 ft 11.5 in); length about 15.65m (51 ft 4.5 in); height 4.55m (14 ft 11.25 in); wing area 52.67m² (566.95 sq ft) including canard foreplanes
Weights: empty about 7,285kg (16,060 lb); loaded about 16,200kg (35,714 lb)
Performance: maximum speed 2,350km/h (1,460 mph); service ceiling 17,000m (55,775 ft); range 768km (477 miles) radius on a hi-lo-hi mission
Armament: two 30mm cannon plus provision for up to 5,775kg (12,731 lb) of disposable stores

Intake-mounted canards distinguish the Cheetah from the original Mirage III design.

British Aerospace Hawk 200

The Hawk 200 is a single-seat attack derivative of the Hawk basic and advanced trainer, and first flew in May 1986. The type uses the volume of the original second cockpit for additional fuel and electronics (including an inertial navigation system), and its nose can be fitted with radar or other sensors (FLIR and/or a laser rangefinder) feeding data to the pilot in a state-of-the-art cockpit fitted with a head-up display.

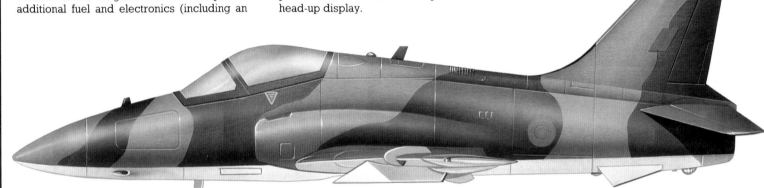

Country of Origin: U.K.
Type: light ground attack and close-support fighter
Crew: one
Power Plant: one Rolls-Royce/Turbomeca Adour Mk 871 non-afterburning turbofan, rated at 26.0kN (5,845 lb) thrust
Dimensions: span 9.39m (30 ft 9.75 in); length 11.38m (37 ft 4 in); height 3.99m (13 ft 1.25 in); wing area 16.69m² (179.6 sq ft)
Weights: empty 4,128kg (9,100 lb); loaded 9,101kg (20,065 lb)
Performance: maximum speed 1,038km/h (645 mph); service ceiling 15,250m (50,030 ft); range 536km (333 miles) radius on a hi-lo-hi mission
Armament: two 25mm Aden cannon plus provision for up to 3,500kg (7,715 lb) of disposable stores

A BAe Hawk 200 demonstrator. Although not purchased by the RAF, the Royal Saudi Arabian Airforce are likely to be the plane's first customer.

British Aerospace Sea Harrier FRS. Mk 1

This is the multi-role carrierborne derivative of the Harrier STOVL close support fighter, and first flew in August 1978 with naval features, a fighter-type cockpit and radar. The type acquitted itself well in the 1982 Falklands War, and is now being upgraded to FRS.Mk 2 standard with more advanced radar, a digital nav/attack system, a revised cockpit of the HOTAS (Hands On Throttle And Stick) type and the latest weapons including two 25mm cannon.

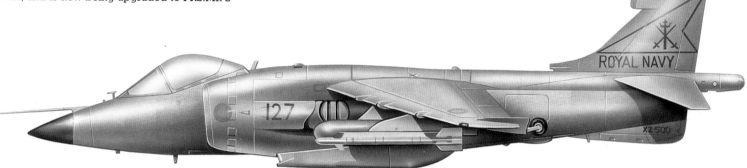

Country of Origin: U.K.
Type: carrierborne STOVL multi-role reconnaissance and strike fighter
Crew: one
Power Plant: one Rolls-Royce Pegasus 11 Mk 104 vectored-thrust non-afterburning turbofan, rated at 95.6kN (21,500 lb) thrust
Dimensions: span 7.70m (25 ft 3 in); length 14.50m (47ft 7 in); height 3.71m (12 ft 2 in); wing area 18.68m² (201.1 sq ft)
Weights: empty 5,942kg (13,100 lb); loaded 11,880kg (26,190 lb)
Performance: maximum speed 1,183km/h (735 mph); service ceiling 15,240+m (50,000+ ft); range 740km (460 miles) radius on a hi-hi-hi mission
Armament: two 30mm cannon plus provision for up to 3,629kg (8,000 lb) of disposable stores

This FRS. Mk2 ordered for the Royal Navy features Blue Vixen radar and new AIM-20 medium-range missiles.

Casa C-101CC Aviojet

First flown in June 1977, the Aviojet is an uncomplicated basic and advanced flying trainer with a useful secondary attack capability. The type is firmly subsonic, but is notably sturdy and possesses excellent range. The initial C-101EB model with the TFE731-2-2J was followed by the C-101BB armed export version with the TFE731-3-1J engine, the C-101CC improved export version, and the C-101DD latest version with more power and an updated electronic suite including a head-up display.

Country of Origin: Spain
Type: basic and advanced flying trainer and weapons trainer with a secondary ground attack capability
Crew: two
Power Plant: one Garrett TFE7315-1J non-afterburning turbofan, rated at 20.91kN (4,700 lb) thrust
Dimensions: span 10.60m (34 ft 9.3 in); length 12.25m (40 ft 2.5 in); height 4.25m (13ft 11.25 in); wing area 20.00m² (215.3 sq ft)
Weights: empty 3,340kg (7,363 lb); loaded 6,300kg (13,889 lb)
Performance: maximum speed 834km/h (518 mph); service ceiling 12,800m (41,995 ft); range 370km (230 miles) radius on a lo-lo-lo mission
Armament: one 30mm cannon or two 12.7mm (0.5 in) machine-guns plus provision for up to 2,250kg (4,460 lb) of disposable stores

A C-101 demonstrating its light attack capability utilizing its underwing weapon stations.

Dassault-Breguet Mirage 50

The Mirage 5 was developed as a clear-weather (and thus radarless) derivative of the Mirage III, and first flew in May 1967. The type has greater fuel capacity and weapon-lifting capability than the Mirage III, while the miniaturization of electronics has allowed later, more powerfully-engined variants such as the Mirage 50 to be fitted with capable attack radar as well as features such as a head-up display and advanced nav/attack system.

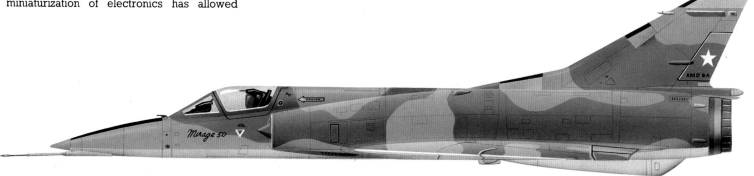

Country of Origin: France
Type: multi-role interceptor and ground attack fighter
Crew: one
Power Plant: one SNECMA Atar 9K-50 afterburning turbojet, rated at 70.6kN (15,873 lb) afterburning thrust
Dimensions: span 8.22m (26 ft 11.5 in); length 15.55m (51 ft 0.25 in); height 4.50m (14 ft 9 in); wing area 35.00m² (376.75 sq ft)
Weights: empty 6,600kg (14,550 lb); loaded 13,700kg (30,200 lb)
Performance: maximum speed 2,350km/h (1,460 mph); service ceiling 17,000m (55,775 ft); range 1,300km (808 miles) radius on a hi-lo-hi mission
Armament: two 30mm cannon plus provision for up to 4,000kg (8,818 lb) of disposable stores

A Mirage III EX. As well as offering new aircraft such as the Mirage 50, the last of the Mirage III family. Dassault-Breguet also rework existing Mirage III airframes incorporating more up-to-date avionics.

Dassault-Breguet Mirage 2000DA

The Mirage 2000 first flew in March 1978 as an advanced fighter of relaxed stability operated by a fly-by-wire control system for optimum performance under all flight regimes. The most important variants are the Mirage 200B two-seat conversion trainer, the Mirage 2000DA air-defence fighter, the Mirage 2000N low-level penetration strike fighter with nuclear weapons, the Mirage 2000N-1 conventionally armed version of the Mirage 2000N, and the Mirage 2000R reconnaissance platform.

Country of Origin: France
Type: interceptor and air-superiority fighter with secondary ground attack capability
Crew: one
Power Plant: one SNECMA M53-P2 afterburning turbojet, rated at 95.1kN (21,385 lb) thrust
Dimensions: span 9.00m (29 ft 6 in); length 14.35m (47 ft 1 in); height 5.30m (17 ft 6 in); wing area 41.00m^2 (441.3 sq ft)
Weights: empty 7,500kg (16,534 lb); loaded 17,000kg (34,478 lb)
Performance: maximum speed 2,350+km/h (1,460+ mph); service ceiling 20,000m (65,615 ft); range 1,480+km (920+ miles) with 1,000kg (2,205 lb) warload
Armament: two 30mm cannon plus provision for up to 6,300 kg (13,889 lb) of disposable stores

A Mirage 2000N two-seater. This Armée de l'Air version is fitted with two Matra 550 Magic missiles.

Dassault-Breguet Mirage F1C

The Mirage F1 was developed as a private venture to succeed the Mirage III, and first flew in December 1966. There have been several variants of this important aircraft, the most significant being the Mirage F1A radarless ground-attack fighter, the Mirage F1B two-seat trainer, the Mirage F1C radar-carrying fighter, the Mirage F1C-200 version of the F1C with an inflight-refuelling probe, the Mirage F1CR-200 probe-fitted reconnaissance platform, and the Mirage F1E export version of the F1C with upgraded electronics.

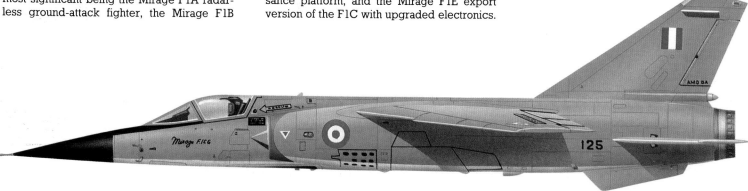

Country of Origin: France
Type: multi-role and ground attack fighter
Crew: one
Power Plant: one SNECMA Atar 9K-50 afterburning turbojet, rated at 70.6kN (15,873 lb) thrust
Dimensions: span 8.40m (27 ft 6.75 in); length 15.00m (49 ft 2.5 in); height 4.50m (14 ft 9 in); wing area 25.00m² (269.1 sq ft)
Weights: empty 7,400kg (16,314 lb); loaded 16,200kg (35,714 lb)
Performance: maximum speed 2,350km/h (1,460 mph); service ceiling 20,000m (65,615 ft); range 425km (224 miles) radius on a hi-lo-hi mission with a 3500kg (7,716 lb) warload
Armament: two 30mm cannon plus plus provision for up to 4,000kg (8,818 lb) of disposable stores

A Mirage F1CR-200 belonging to the Escadre de Reconnaissance 33 of the Armée de l'Air.

Dassault-Breguet Rafale-A

From the Rafale-A demonstrator that first flew in July 1986, Dassault-Breguet is developing a slightly smaller and lighter service type that will be built in Rafale-D air force and Rafale-M navy variants. The fighters will embody relaxed stability, a digital fly-by-wire control system, a reclining pilot's seat, a wide-angle head-up display, a large measure of composites in the structure, SNECMA M88 turbofans and provision for the retrofit of fibre-optic, voice command and voice warning systems.

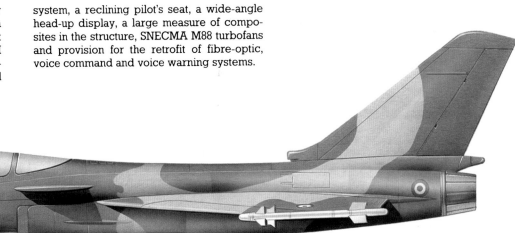

Country of Origin: France
Type: multi-role tactical fighter demonstrator
Crew: one
Power Plant: two General Electric F404-GE-400 afterburning turbofans, rated at 71.2kN (16,000 lb) thrust each
Dimensions: span 11.00m (36 ft 1 in); length 15.80 m (51 ft 10 in); height not available; wing area 47.00m² (505.92 sq ft).
Weights: empty 9,250 kg (20,932 lb); loaded 20,000kg (44,092 lb)
Performance: maximum speed 2,125+km/h (1,320+ mph); service ceiling not available; range 600km (373 miles) radius with a 3,500kg (7,716 lb) warload on a hi-lo-hi mission
Armament: one 30mm cannon plus provision for disposable stores up to an unstated weight

The Rafale-A carrying two wingtip-mounted Matra Magic and four Matra Mica medium-range air-to-air missiles.

Dassault-Breguet Super Etendard

This ungraded development of the Etendard carrierborne fighter first flew in June 1978 with refinements to produce true transonic performance, more power, provision for the Exocet anti-ship missile, and search radar in a revised nose. Some 50 of the 71 aircraft are being modified with Anemone radar in place of the standard Agave equipment and an inertial navigation system for low-level penetration with the ASMP nuclear-tipped stand-off missile.

Country of Origin: France
Type: carrierborne and land-based attack and strike fighter
Crew: one
Power Plant: one SNECMA Atar 8K-50 non-afterburning turbojet, rated at 49kN (11,023 lb) thrust
Dimensions: span 9.60m (31 ft 6 in); length 14.31m (46 ft 11.5 in); height 3.86m (12 ft 8 in); wing area 24.80m² (267.00 sq ft)
Weights: empty 6,500kg (14,330 lb); loaded 12,000kg (26,455 lb)
Performance: maximum speed 1,180km/h (733 mph); service ceiling 13,700m (44,950 ft); range 850km (528 miles) radius with one AM.39 Exocet missile
Armament: two 30mm cannon plus provision for up to 2,100kg (4,630 lb) of disposable stores

The first Super Etendard prototype was constructed from a standard Etendard IV and fitted with Nav/attack system and Agave radar.

Dassault-Breguet/ Dornier Alpha Jet 1

The Alpha Jet was designed to provide the French with an advanced trainer (formerly Alpha Jet E), and the West Germans with a close-support fighter (formerly Alpha Jet A), and first flew in October 1973. These Alpha Jet 1s were complemented from 1982 by the Alpha Jet 2 close-support and limited air-combat version, and from 1985 by the Alpha Jet 3 with radar and more advanced weapons. The latest variant is the Alpha Jet Advanced Training System based on the Alpha Jet 3 with a state-of-the-art cockpit.

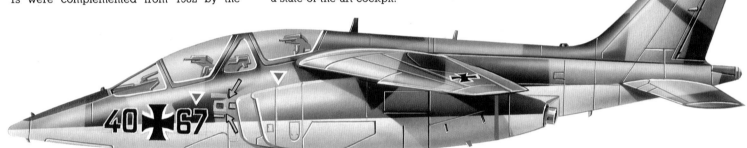

Countries of Origin: France and West Germany
Type: multi-role light ground attack and advanced jet trainer
Crew: two
Power Plant: two Turbomeca Larzac 04-C6 non-afterburning turbofans, rated at 13.24kN (2,976 lb) thrust each
Dimensions: span 9.11m (29 ft 10.75 in); length 13.23m (43 ft 5 in); height 4.19m (13 ft 9 in); wing area 17.50m² (188.4 sq ft)
Weights: empty 3,515kg (7,749 lb); loaded 8,000kg (17,637 lb)
Performance: maximum speed 1,000km/h (621 mph); service ceiling 14,630m (48,000 ft); range 583km (363 miles) radius on a hi-lo-hi mission with maximum warload
Armament: one 27mm cannon plus provision for up to 2,500kg (5,511 lb) of disposable stores

An Alpha Jet 2 configured here in a maritime strike role and carrying an Exocet anti-ship missile and two Matra Magic air-to-air missiles.

Eurofighter EFA

Based ultimately on the British Aerospace EAP demonstrator that first flew in August 1986, the EFA is being developed by Italy, Spain, the U.K. and West Germany as a multi-role fighter slightly larger and heavier than the French Rafale but sharing the same design and structural concepts as a delta-winged type with canard foreplanes, relaxed stability and digital fly-by-wire control system. The prototype should fly in 1991, with aircraft beginning to enter service in 1996 with Eurojet EJ.200 engines.

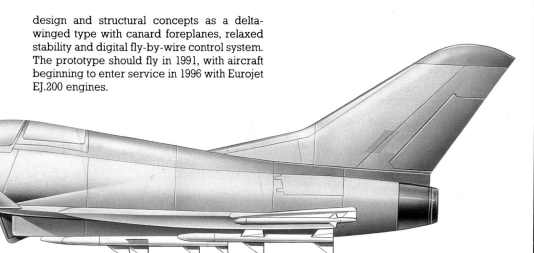

Countries of Origin: Italy, Spain, U.K. and West Germany
Type: air defence fighter, with secondary ground attack capability
Crew: one
Power Plant: two Eurojet EJ200 advanced technology afterburning turbofans, rated at 90kN (20,250 lb) thrust each
Dimensions: span 10.50m (34 ft 5.5 in); length 14.50m (47ft 7.0 in); height not available; wing area not available
Weights: empty 9,750kg (21,495 lb); loaded 17,000kg (37,480 lb)
Performance: maximum speed 2,200km/h (1,368 mph); service ceiling not available; range 556km (345 miles) with typical war load
Armament: (fighter) one cannon plus up to 4,500kg (9,920 lb) of air-to-air missiles

The artwork above shows British Aerospace's EAP aircraft which is the technology demonstrator for the EFA, a mock-up of which is shown in the photograph on the right.

Fairchild Republic A-10A Thunderbolt II

First flown in May 1972, this aircraft is dedicated to the close air support and anti-tank roles with firmly subsonic performance from an airframe optimized for survivability over the battlefield through armour protection, separation and/or concealment of vulnerable features, and the redundancy of vital systems.

Sophisticated electronics are not fitted, but it carries the world's most powerful multi-barrel cannon for anti-tank operations, complemented by a wide assortment of external stores including six AGM-65 Maverick air-to-surface missiles.

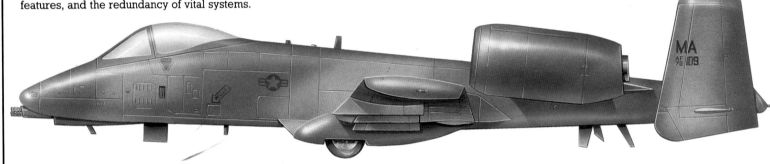

Country of Origin: U.S.A.
Type: anti-tank and battlefield close support aircraft
Crew: one
Power Plant: two General Electric TF34-GE-100 non-afterburning turbofans, rated at 40.3kN (9,065 lb) thrust each
Dimensions: span 17.53m (57 ft 6 in); length 16.26m (53 ft 4 in); height 4.47m (14 ft 8 in); wing area 47.01m² (506.00 sq ft)
Weights: empty 11,322kg (24,960 lb); loaded 22,680kg (50,000 lb)
Performance: maximum speed 706km/h (439 mph); service ceiling not stated; range 463km (288 miles) radius on a lo-lo-lo mission with a 1-hour loiter
Armament: one 30mm GAU-8/A Avenger 30mm/seven-barrel cannon plus provision for up to 7,258kg (16,000 lb) of disposable stores

The 'Warthog', as the A-10 is popularly known, generating wingtip vortices in a low-altitude, high-g turn.

General Dynamics
F-16C Fighting Falcon

The F-16 is the West's most important air-combat fighter, and first flew in February 1974 as a lightweight fighter demonstrator with a fly-by-wire control system after the Vietnam War had revealed the tactical shortcomings of heavyweight fighters with excellent outright performance but inadequate reliability and agility. The original F-16A single-seat and F-16B two-seat variants have been supplemented since 1984 by the F-16C and F-16D equivalents with important electronic and aerodynamic improvements.

Country of Origin: U.S.A.
Type: multi-role air-combat and ground attack fighter
Crew: one
Power Plant: one Pratt & Whitney F100-PW-220 afterburning turbofan, rated at 104.3kN (23,450 lb) thrust
Dimensions: span 9.45m (31 ft 0 in); length 15.09m (49 ft 4.9 in); height 5.09m (16 ft 8.5 in); wing area 27.87m² (300.00 sq ft)
Weights: empty 7,618kg (16,795 lb); loaded 17,010kg (37,500 lb)
Performance: maximum speed 2125+km/h (1,320+ mph); service ceiling 18,000+m (59,055+ ft); range 925+km (575+ miles) radius on a hi-lo-hi mission
Armament: one 20mm M61A1 Vulcan six-barrel cannon plus provision typically for up to 5,413kg (11,935 lb) of disposable stores

An F-16C of USAF's 17th Tactical Fighter Squadron, maneuvering into position to be refuelled by a KC-10A Extender aircraft.

Grumman
F-14A Tomcat

The Tomcat is the world's most powerful fighter, a carrierborne type that first flew in December 1970 as an air-defence type with variable-geometry wings, the potent AWG-9 radar fire-control system and a primary armament of up to six AIM-54 Phoenix long-range air-to-air missiles. Many in-service F-14As are to be reworked to F-14A (Plus) standard with the more reliable and powerful General Electric F110-GE-400 turbofans, but in 1989 the F-14D with these engines and a host of electronic improvements was cancelled for budgetary reasons.

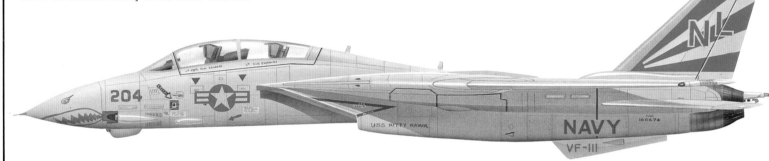

Country of Origin: U.S.A.
Type: carrierborne long-range air-defence fighter
Crew: two
Power Plant: two Pratt & Whitney TF30-P-412A afterburning turbofans, rated at 93kN (20,900 lb) thrust each
Dimensions: span 19.54m (64 ft 1.5 in) spread and 11.65m (38 ft 2.5 in) swept; length 19.10m (62 ft 8 in); height 4.88m (16 ft 0 in); wing area 52.49m² (565.00 sq ft) spread
Weights: empty 18,191kg (40,104 lb); loaded 33,724kg (74,348 lb)
Performance: maximum speed 2,486km/h (1,545 mph); service ceiling 15,240+m (50,000+ ft); range 3,219km (2,000 miles) with maximum fuel
Armament: one 20mm M61A1 Vulcan six-barrel cannon plus provision for up to 6,577kg (14,500 lb) of disposable stores

An F-14A of the US Navy's Fighter Squadron 84 ('Jolly Rogers') based on the USS Nimitz, armed with Sidewinder and Sparrow air-to-air missiles.

Israel Aircraft Industries Kfir-C7

When the delivery of its Mirage 5s was embargoed in 1967 by France, Israel pushed forward with its own development of the basic Mirage III airframe to produce the Atar-engined Nesher and ultimately the Kfir with the U.S. J79 engine. The first Kfir C1 flew in 1971, and since then several increasingly advanced derivatives have been produced as the Kfir-C2 and two-seat Kfir-TC2 with canard foreplanes, updated in the definitive Kfir-C7 and Kfir-TC7 versions with more modern electronics and an uprated engine.

Country of Origin: Israel
Type: multi-role interceptor and ground attack fighter
Crew: one
Power Plant: one General Electric J79-GE-J1E afterburning turbojet, rated at 83.41kN (18,750 lb) thrust
Dimensions: span 8.22m (26 ft 11.5 in); length 15.65m (51 ft 4.5 in); height 4.55m (14 ft 11.25 in); wing area 36.46m² (392.47 sq ft) including canard foreplanes
Weights: empty 7,300kg (16,093 lb); loaded 16,500kg (36,376 lb)
Performance: maximum speed 2335km/h (1,450 mph); service ceiling 17,700m (58,070 ft); range 535km (330 miles) on a hi-hi-hi interception mission
Armament: two 30mm cannon plus provision for up to 6,085kg (13,415 lb) of disposable stores

Three Israeli Air Force Kfir ('Young Lion') flying in close formation.

Lockheed F-117A

The world's first operational 'stealth' airplane, the F-117A first flew in 1981 but was only revealed in 1988. It had originally been thought to be a 'blended' design like the SR-71, but is now known to be a highly angular type with a short central nacelle ending in a butterfly tail, the whole layout being intended to trap enemy radar emissions and so produce no echo. The type is optimized for the penetration of enemy airspace to 'take out' key targets. Its missiles are housed internally by two weapons bays. The USAF is believed to have ordered 59 F-117s, of which 52 have been delivered. Three of the F-117s are known to have crashed. Security on the aircraft has now been partly lifted because the aircraft's technology has been overshadowed by the Northrop B-2 stealth bomber.

Country of Origin: U.S.A.
Type: 'stealth' penetration strike fighter
Crew: one
Power Plant: two General Electric F404 non-afterburning turbofans, rated at 53.4kN (12,000 lb) thrust each
Dimensions: span 11.58m (38 ft 0 in); length between 7.315m and 7.92m (24 ft 0 in and 26 ft 0 in); height between 3.66m and 4.88m (12 ft 0 in and 16 ft 0 in); wing area not revealed
Weights: empty 6,804kg (15,000 lb); loaded 13,608kg (30,000 lb)
Performance: maximum speed high subsonic; service ceiling not available; range 805km (500 miles) combat radius
Armament: up to 907kg (2,000 lb) of anti-radar missiles or other 'smart' weapons
Note: All data are provisional

McDonnell Douglas F-15C Eagle

The F-15 is the air-superiority counterpart to the F-16 and, developed as successor to the F-4 Phantom II, first flew in July 1972 and immediately displayed outstanding performance especially in speed and climb. The initial F-15A and two-seat F-15B variants were complemented from 1985 by the equivalent F-15C and F-15D models with conformal fuel tanks and electronic improvements, and the F-15E that is entering service is the interdiction version of the F-15D. The F-15E has a restressed and strengthened structure giving it double the life of earlier Eagles. Its mission computer and electronic warfare equipment have also been upgraded.

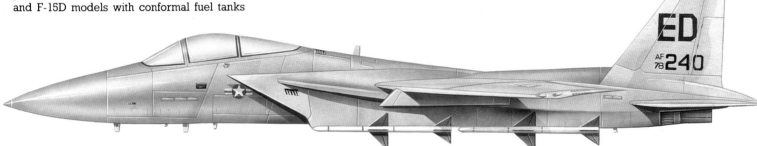

Country of Origin: U.S.A.
Type: air-superiority and ground attack fighter
Crew: one
Power Plant: two Pratt & Whitney F100-P-100 afterburning turbofans, rated at 106.6kN (23,950 lb) thrust each
Dimensions: span 13.05m (42 ft 9.75 in); length 19.43m (63 ft 9 in); height 5.63m (18 ft 5.5 in); wing area 56.48m² (608.00 sq ft)
Weights: empty 12,247kg (27,000 lb); loaded 30,845kg (68,000 lb)
Performance: maximum speed, 2,655+km/h (1,650+ mph); service ceiling 18,290m (60,000 ft); range 1,968m (1,223 miles) radius on a hi-hi-hi mission
Armament: one 20mm M61A1 Vulcan cannon plus provision for up to 8,165+kg (18,000+ lb) of disposable stores

An F-15 Eagle of the 1st Tactical Fighter Wing being deployed to Riyadh, Saudi Arabia.

McDonnell Douglas F/A-18C Hornet

Developed from Northrop's losing lightweight fighter competitor to the F-16, the F/A-18 was developed as a larger dual-role aircraft and first flew in November 1979. The type offers advanced aerodynamics and a combination of the very best avionics and sensors to make it formidable in both its primary roles. The initial F/A-18A and two-seat F/A-18B variants were supplemented from 1987 by the F/A-18C upgraded single-seater and F/A-18C two-seater optimized for the night attack role. An RF-18D reconnaissance variant is under development.

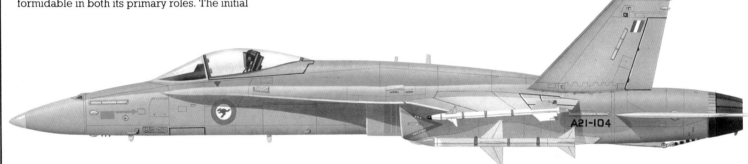

Country of Origin: U.S.A.
Type: carrierborne and land-based multi-role fighter and ground attack aircraft
Crew: one
Power Plant: two General Electric F404-GE-400 afterburning turbofans, rated at 71.2kN (16,000 lb) thrust each
Dimensions: span 11.43m (37 ft 6 in); length 17.07m (56 ft 0 in); height 4.66m (15 ft 3.5 in); wing area 37.16m² (400.00 sq ft)
Weights: empty 10,406kg (23,060 lb); loaded 22,320kg (49,205 lb)
Performance: maximum speed 1,915+ km/h (1,190+ mph); service ceiling 15,240m (50,000 ft); range 740+ km (460+ miles) on a hi-hi-hi mission
Armament: one 20mm M61A1 Vulcan cannon plus provision for 8,165kg (18,000 lb) of disposable stores

An F/A-18A Hornet taking off from the flight deck of the USS Constellation.

McDonnell Douglas/British Aerospace AV-8B Harrier II

This is a radical development of the Harrier with an all-composite wing of larger area and supercritical section fitted with leading-edge root extensions, flaps and drooping ailerons, which with the enhanced lift-improvement devices and more powerful engine greatly increases warload without sacrifice of range.

The type has several other improvements including a fighter-type cockpit and more advanced electronics, and serves with the British as the Harrier GR.Mk 5. A night-attack capability is being added, British machines with this capability currently unofficially known as Harrier GR.Mk 7s.

Country of Origin: U.K. and U.S.A.
Type: STOVL close-support aircraft
Crew: one
Power Plant: one Rolls-Royce F402-R-406 (Pegasus 11-21) vectored-thrust non-afterburning turbofan, rated at 97.9kN (22,000 lb) thrust
Dimensions: span 9.25m (30 ft 4 in); length 14.12m (46 ft 4 in); height 3.55m (11 ft 7.75 in); wing area 21.37m² (230.00 sq ft)
Weights: empty 6,783kg (12,750 lb); loaded 14,100kg (31,085 lb)
Performance: maximum speed 1,020+km/h (634+ mph); service ceiling 13,700+m (44,950+ ft); range 282km (172 miles) radius on a lo-lo-lo mission with a 2,722kg (6,000 lb) warload
Armament: one 25mm GAU-12/U Equalizer six-barrel cannon or (British aircraft) two 25mm Aden cannon plus provision for up to 7,711kg (17,000 lb) of disposable stores

The night attack version of the AV-8B for the US Marine Corp.

McDonnell Douglas/Israel Aircraft Industries Phantom 2000

This is an Israeli reworking of the F-4E Phantom II and started to enter service in 1989 to provide a viable operational capability into the next century. The type has a number of structural and electrical upgrades, but more importantly new radar and electronic countermeasures plus a completely modernized cockpit with head-down displays and a wide-angle head-up display plus HOTAS (Hands On Throttle And Stick) controls.

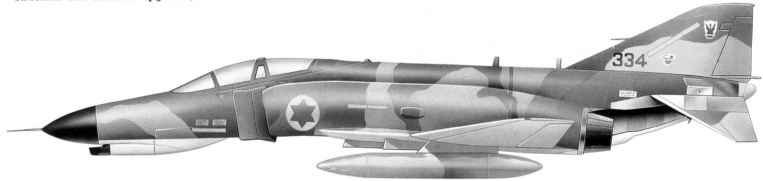

Country of Origin: Israel
Type: multi-role interceptor and ground attack fighter
Crew: two
Power Plant: two General Electric J79-GE-17 afterburning turbojets, rated at 79.65kN (17,9000 lb) thrust each
Dimensions: span 11.77m (38 ft 7.5 in); length 19.20m (63 ft 0 in); height 5.02m (16 ft 5.5 in); wing area 49.24m² (530.00 sq ft)
Weights: not available
Performance: maximum speed 2,301 km/h (1,430 mph); service ceiling 17,905m (58,750 ft); range 1,145km (712 miles) radius on a hi-lo-hi interdiction mission
Armament: one 20mm M61A1 Vulcan six-barrel cannon plus provision for up to 7,257kg (16,000 lb) of disposable stores

An IAI Super Phantom, a re-engined F-4, powered in this case by two P/W 1120 engines leaves the runway on its first flight.

Mikoyan-Gurevich MiG-21BIS 'Fishbed-L'

Now obsolescent but in its time one of the world's most important fighters, the MiG-21 first few in early 1957, and was built in large numbers in many variants. The first series (up to the 'Fishbed-F') are day fighters with the R-11 turbojet, the second series (up to the 'Fishbed-J') are dual-role fighters with the R-13 turbojet, and the definitive third series ('Fishbed-N') is a limited multi-role fighter with the R-25 turbojet.

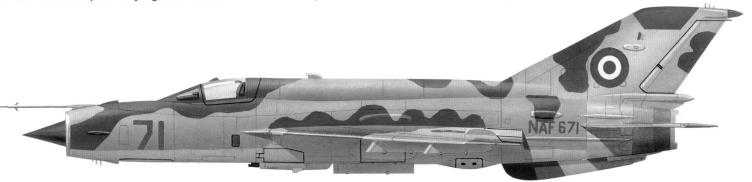

Country of Origin: U.S.S.R
Type: interceptor and ground-attack fighter
Crew: one
Power Plant: one Tumanskii R-13-300 afterburning turbojet, rated at 64.7kN (14,550 lb) thrust
Dimensions: span 7.15m (23 ft 5.5 in); length 15.76m (51 ft 8.5 in); height 4.10m (13 ft 5.5 in); wing area 23.00m² (247.58 sq ft)
Weights: empty 5,715kg (12,599 lb); loaded 9,400kg (20,723 lb)
Performance: maximum speed 2,230km/h (1,386 mph); service ceiling 17,800m (58,400 ft); range 1,100km (683 miles)
Armament: one 23mm GSh-23L twin-barrel cannon plus provision for 1,500kg (3,307 lb) of disposable stores

A MiG-21 of the Finnish Air Force. Though the aircraft lacked the payload of the Phantom II and the performance of the F-15 it is still a threat when well-handled.

Mikoyan-Gurevich MiG-23MG 'Flogger-G'

The MiG-23 was produced as successor to the MiG-21 with variable-geometry wings to optimize field and flight performance. The type first flew in 1966, and the pro-production type used the Lyul'ka AL-5 turbojet that was ex- changed for the Tumanskii R-27 and later R-29 in the increasingly capable production variants that have now reached the 'Flogger-K' model.

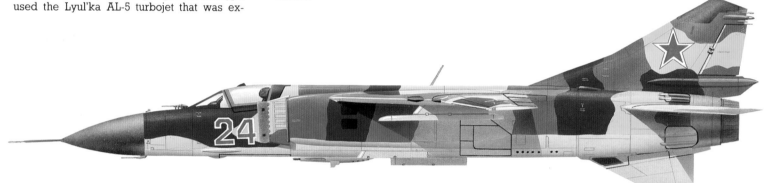

Country of Origin: U.S.S.R.

Type: multi-role and air-combat fighter

Crew: one

Power Plant: one Tumanskii R-29B afterburning turbojet, rated at 122kN (27,500 lb) afterburning thrust

Dimensions: span 14.25m (46 ft 9 in) spread and 8.30m (27 ft 2 in) swept; length 18.25m (59 ft 10 in); height 4.35m (14 ft 4 in); wing area 37.20m² (400.43 sq ft)

Weights: empty 11,300kg (24,912 lb); loaded 18,500kg (40,785 lb)

Performance: maximum speed 2,500km/h (1,553 mph); service ceiling 18,300m (60,040 ft); range 930km (575 miles) on a hi-hi-hi mission

Armament: one 23mm GSh-23L twin-barrel cannon plus provision for up to 3,000kg (6,614 lb) of disposable stores

A MiG-23 carrying a centre-line fuel tank and with its wings fully swept.

Mikoyan-Gurevich
MiG-25M 'Foxbat-E'

The MiG-25 was designed to counter the North American B-70 Valkyrie Mach 3 strategic bomber, but was kept in development after the cancellation of the American machine. First flown in 1964 or 1965, the type entered service in 'Foxbat-A' interceptor, 'Foxbat-B' and 'Foxbat-D' reconnaissance, and 'Foxbat-C' two-seat trainer variants. Most 'Foxbat-As' have been converted to 'Foxbat-E' standard for lower-altitude operations with more power, a new radar and a revised weapons fit.

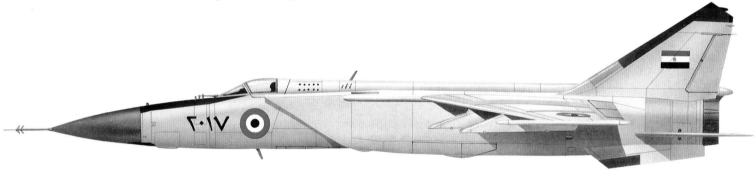

Country of Origin: U.S.S.R.
Type: interceptor fighter
Crew: two
Power Plant: two Tumanskii R-31F afterburning turbojets, rated at 136.5kN (30,684 lb) thrust each
Dimensions: span 13.95m (45 ft 9 in); length 23.82m (78 ft 1.75 in); height 6.10m (20 ft 0.25 in); wing area 56.83m² (611.7 sq ft)
Weights: empty 20,000kg (44,092 lb); loaded 37,500kg (82,672 lb)
Performance: maximum speed 2,975km/h (1,849 mph); service ceiling 24,400m (80,050 ft); range 1,130km (702 miles) radius on a hi-hi-hi mission
Armament: one cannon of unstated calibre plus provision for up to 2,000kg (4,409 lb) of disposable stores

Two MiG-25s of the Soviet Air Force, each carrying two pairs of AA-6 Acrid air-to-air missiles, the largest such missiles in the world.

Mikoyan-Gurevich MiG-27 'Flogger-D'

The MiG-27 was developed from the MiG-23 as a dedicated ground-attack fighter with fixed inlets, a two-position nozzle and a completely revised and armoured forward fuselage without air-search radar but with specialist sensors and good downward fields of vision. The type first flew in 1970, and has been produced in 'Flogger-D' and 'Flogger-J' variants, while the 'Flogger-F' and 'Flogger-H' are MiG-23/27 hybrids for export.

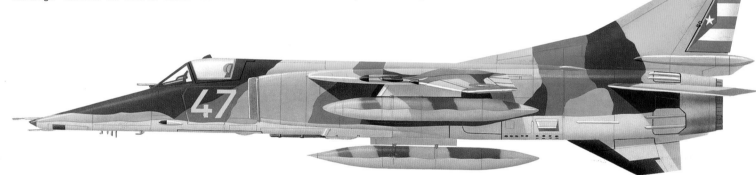

Country of Origin: U.S.S.R.
Type: ground-attack fighter
Crew: one
Power Plant: one Tumanskii R-29B afterburning turbojet, rated at 112.8kN (25,353 lb) thrust
Dimensions: span 14.25m (46 ft 9 in) spread and 8.17m (26 ft 9.7 in) swept; length 16.00m (52 ft 5.9 in); height 4.35m (14 ft 3.3 in); wing area 27.26m² (293.43 sq ft)
Weights: empty 10,790kg (23,778 lb); loaded 20,100kg (44,313 lb)
Performance: maximum speed 1,807km/h (1,123 mph); service ceiling 16,000m (52,495 ft); range 390km (242 miles) radius on a lo-lo-lo mission
Armament: one 23mm six-barrel cannon plus provision for up to 4,000kg (8,818 lb) of disposable stores

This 'Flogger-J' variant of the MiG-27, introduced in 1983, has a lengthened nose and wing leading-edge extension.

Mikoyan-Gurevich MiG-29 'Fulcrum-A'

The MiG-29 began to enter service in 1985 as partial replacement for the MiG-23, and can be likened in configuration to a McDonnell Douglas F-15 scaled down to the size of the same company's F/A-18. The type possesses great agility and capable electronics, but is also notable for its retention of a mechanical control system. The 'Fulcram-A' baseline single-seater is complemented by the 'Fulcrum-B' two-seater and the electronically upgraded 'Fulcrum-C' single-seater.

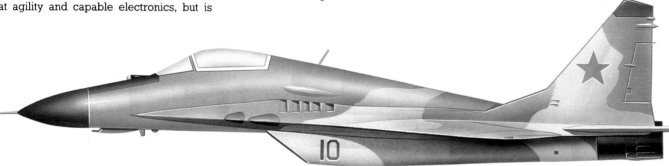

Country of Origin: U.S.S.R.
Type: air-superiority and ground attack fighter
Crew: one
Power Plant: two Tumanskii R-33D afterburning turbofans, rated at 81.4kN (18,298 lb) thrust each
Dimensions: span 11.36m (37 ft 3.25 in); length 17.32m (56 ft 9.85 in); height 4.73m (15 ft 6.2 in); wing area 35.50m² (382.13 sq ft)
Weights: empty 7,825kg (17,251 lb); loaded 18,000kg (39,683 lb)
Performance: maximum speed 2,445+km/h (1,519+ mph); service ceiling 17,000m (55,775 ft); range 1,150km (715 miles) radius on a hi-hi-hi mission
Armament: one 23mm GSh-23L twin-barrel cannon plus provision for disposable stores up to an unstated weight

A plan view of an airborne MiG-29. Like many recent US designs the 'Fulcrum' features twin vertical stabilizers.

Mitsubishi F-1

This trim airplane bears more than a passing resemblance to the SEPECAT Jaguar in layout and role (including supersonic training in its T-2 baseline form), and is powered by the same basic engine. The T-2 first flew in July 1971, being followed in June 1975 by the F-1 with the rear cockpit volume devoted to additional electronics such as the intertial navigation system, electronic countermeasurers system and attack computer.

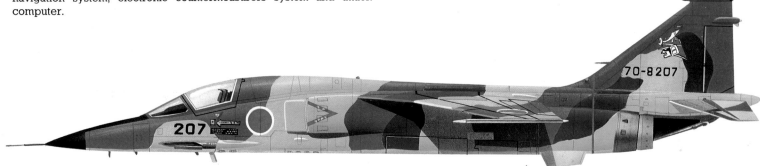

Country of Origin: Japan
Type: close support fighter
Crew: one
Power Plant: two Ishikawajima-Harima TF40-IHI-801A (Rolls-Royce/Turbomeca Adour Mk 801A) afterburning turbofans, rated at 3,207kg (7,070 lb) thrust each
Dimensions: span 7.88m (25 ft 10.25 in); length 17.84m (58 ft 6.25 in); height 4.28m (14 ft 4.25 in); wing area 21.18m² (227.99 sq ft)
Weights: empty 6,358kg (14,017 lb); loaded 13,675kg (30,148 lb)
Performance: maximum speed 1,700km/h (1,056 mph); service ceiling 15,240m (50,000 ft); range 555km (345 mile) on a hi-lo-hi mission
Armament: one 20mm JM61A1 Vulcan six-barrel cannon plus provision for up to 2,780kg (6,129 lb) of disposable stores

Two Japanese Air Self Defence Force F-1 aircraft in formation with a 12th Tactical Fighter Squadron F-15 Eagle during a joint exercise.

Northrop F-5E Tiger II

First flown in March 1969, this is a development of the F-5A Freedom Fighter with aerodynamic refinements and more power for significantly greater agility, performance and payload. The type also carries radar plus an integrated fire-control system and more advanced weapons. The F-5E single-seater is complemented by the F-5B combat-capable two-seater and the RF-5E Tigereye reconnaissance platform.

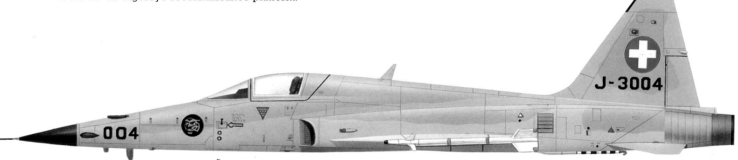

Country of Origin: U.S.A.
Type: lightweight tactical fighter
Crew: one
Power Plant: two General Electric J85-GE-21 afterburning turbojets, rated at 22.25kN (5,000 lb) thrust each
Dimensions: span 8.13m (26 ft 8 in); length 14.73m (47 ft 4.75 in); height 4.08m (13 ft 4.5 in); wing area 17.28m² (186.00 sq ft)
Weights: empty 4,410kg (9,723 lb); loaded 11,214kg (24,722 lb)
Performance: maximum speed 1,743km/h (1,083 mph); service ceiling 15,850m (52,000 ft); range 305km (190 miles) radius with a 2,857kg (6,300 lb) warload
Armament: two 20mm cannon plus provision for up to 3,175kg (7,000 lb) of disposable stores

Two F5-E Tiger IIs. These aircraft have been purchased by many nations worldwide. USAF utilize theirs in an aggressor training role.

Panavia Tornado ADV

Developed as a long-range interdiction and strike aircraft for three Western European nations, the Tornado is a variable-geometry STOL type with very high performance at low level, allowing first-pass delivery of weapons with great accuracy. The baseline Tornado IDS flew in April 1974, and has been joined by the Tornado ADV air-defence variant with a longer fuselage plus specialist radar and weapons, and the Tornado ECR for electronic warfare and reconnaissance.

Countries of Origin: Italy, U.K. and West Germany
Type: long-range air-defence fighter
Crew: two
Power Plant: two Turbo-Union RB199-34R Mk 104 afterburning turbofans, rated at 72.5kN (16,290 lb) thrust each
Dimensions: span 13.91m (45 ft 7.5 in) spread and 8.60m (28 ft 2.5 in) swept; length 18.06m (59 ft 3 in); height 5.70m (18 ft 8.4 in); wing area 25.00m² (269.11 sq ft)
Weights: empty 14,500kg (31,965 lb); loaded 27,987kg (61,700 lb)
Performance: maximum speed 2,340km/h (1,454 mph); service ceiling 21,300+m (69,880+ ft); range 740+km (460+ miles) radius on a hi-hi-hi mission
Armament: one 27mm cannon plus provision for up to 8,500kg (18,740 lb) of disposable stores

A Tornado F-3 of 29 Squadron Royal Air Force.

Saab-Scania JA 37 Viggen

The Viggen first flew in February 1971, and is a substantial multi-role type that nevertheless secures STOL performance through its combination of candard layout and powerful reversible-thrust turbofan. The initial version was the AJ 37 attack model, and this was followed by SF 37 overland reconnaissance, SH 37 overwater reconnaissance and SK 37 two-seat models before the advent of the JA 37 dedicated air-defence fighter with an inbuilt cannon, more advanced radar and greater power.

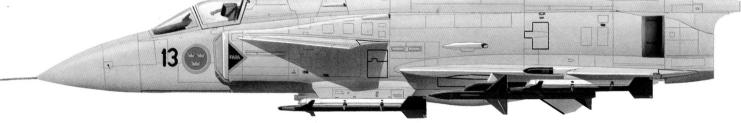

Country of Origin: Sweden
Type: all-weather interceptor with secondary ground attack capability
Crew: one
Power Plant: one Volvo Flygmotor RM8B (developed Pratt & Whitney JT8D-22) afterburning turbofan, rated at 125kN (28,108 lb) thrust
Dimensions: span 10.60m (34 ft 9.25 in); length 16.40m (53 ft 9.75 in); height 5.90m (19 ft 4.25 in); wing area 52.20m² (561.89 sq ft) including canard foreplanes
Weights: empty not available; loaded 20,500kg (45,194 lb)
Performance: maximum speed 2,125+km/h (1,320+ mph); service ceiling 15,200+m (49,870+ ft); range 1,000km (621 miles) radius on a hi-lo-hi mission
Armament: one 30mm cannon plus provision for 6,000kg (13,228 lb) of disposable stores

The Swedes utilize public roads for the operation of their fighters.

Saab-Scania JAS 39 Gripen

The JAS 39 is an interesting effort to break away from the mould of ever larger and heavier fighters, and is an aerodynamically advanced canard design with relaxed stability and a fly-by-wire control system. The airframe has a large measure of composites in its structure, and the electronics are notably comprehensive. The first example flew in 1989 but was then lost in an accident caused by software problems in the flight control system.

Country of Origin: Sweden
Type: multi-role fighter, with ground attack and reconnaissance capability
Crew: one
Power Plant: one Volvo Flygmotor RM12 (developed General Electric F404) afterburning turbofan, rated at 80.1kN (18,000 lb) thrust
Dimensions: span 8.00m (26 ft 3 in); length 14.00m (45 ft 11.2 in); height 4.70m (15 ft 5 in); wing area not available
Weights: empty not available; loaded 11,350kg (25,022 lb)
Performance: maximum speed 2,128km/h (1,323 mph); service ceiling not available; range not available
Armament: one 27mm cannon plus provision for up to 6,500kg (14,330 lb) of disposable stores

An air-to-air photo of a Grippen prototype. Despite the crash of the prototype the Swedish Air Force has ordered some 400.

Sepecat Jaguar GR.Mk 1

This Anglo-French aircraft was schemed initially as a supersonic trainer (British Jaguar B and French Jaguar E), but by the time it first flew in September 1968 its anticipated capabilities led to the decision to use it mainly as a single-seat attack fighter (French Jaguar A and British Jaguar S). The type has no radar, but a capable nav/attack system based on an inertial navigation system and laser ranger/market-target seeker. The Jaguar International export version can be fitted with Agave radar for the missile-armed anti-ship role.

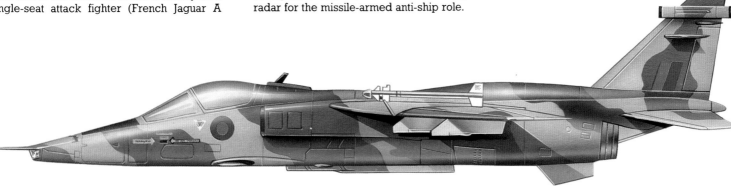

Countries of Origin: France and U.K.
Type: strike, close support and reconnaissance fighter
Crew: one
Power Plant: two Rolls-Royce/Turbomeca Adour Mk 104 afterburning turbofans, rated at 35.78kN (8,040 lb) thrust each
Dimensions: span 8.69m (28 ft 6 in); length 16.83m (55 ft 2.5 in); height 4.89m (16 ft 0.5 in); wing area 24.18m² (260.27 sq ft)
Weights: empty 7,000kg (15,430 lb); loaded 15,700kg (34,610 lb)
Performance: maximum speed 1,700km/h (1,056 mph); service ceiling 14,020m (46,000 ft); range 537km (334 miles) radius on a lo-lo-lo mission
Armament: two 30mm cannon plus provision for up to 4,763kg (10,500 lb) of disposable stores

A Jaguar of No 6 Squadron based at RAF Coltishall with a laser-guided bomb on centre line, 2×1200 litre fuel tanks inboard and 2 Sidewinder AIM 9L missiles on outer wing stations.

Shenyang J-6C 'Farmer'

This is the Chinese version of the MiG-19 'Farmer' fighter, and though obsolescent in overall terms still retains a useful air-combat capability because of its combination of modest performance with excellent agility and powerful cannon armament. Deliveries began in late 1961, and the type has the export designation F-6. Four fighter variants have been produced (including one with radar) as well as a reconnaissance platform and a two-seat trainer.

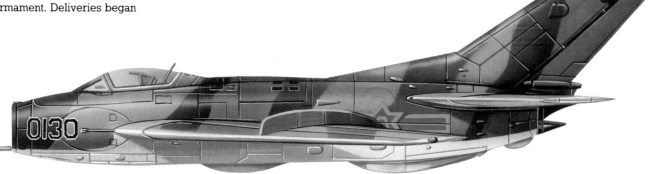

Country of Origin: China
Type: air-combat fighter
Crew: one
Power Plant: two Wopen WP-6 (Tumanskii R-9BF-811) afterburning turbojets, rated at 31.88kN (7,165 lb) thrust each
Dimensions: span 9.20m (30 ft 2.25 in); length 12.60m (41 ft 4 in); height 3.88m (12 ft 8.75 in); wing area 25.00m² (269.11 sq ft)
Weights: empty 5,670kg (12,700 lb); loaded 8,965kg (19,764 lb)
Performance: maximum speed 1,540km/h (957 mph); service ceiling 17,900m (58,725 ft); range 685km (426 miles) radius on a hi-hi-hi mission
Armament: three 30mm cannon plus provision for up to 500kg (1,102 lb) of disposable stores

The photograph shows a Syrian Air Force MiG-19 from which the Shenyang J-6 was developed.

Shenyang J-8-1 'Finback'

While building its Xian J-7 version of the MiG-21, China also used the basic concept as the basis of the J-8, which has wing-root inlets to allow the nose to be used for powerful search radar. The airframe is scaled-up from that of the X-7, and a twin-engined power plant is used. The type was developed in the 1960s, and the J-8-II that first flew in 1984 with more powerful WP-13A-ii (R-13-300) engine is to be fitted with US electronics to create a more capable machine.

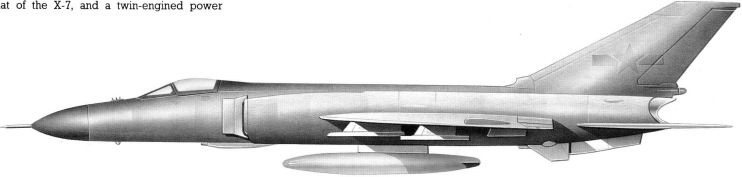

Country of Origin: China
Type: air-superiority fighter with secondary ground attack capability
Crew: one
Power Plant: two Wopen WP-7 (Tumanskii R-11) afterburning turbojets, rated at 60.82kN (13,668 lb) thrust each
Dimensions: span 10.00m (32 ft 9.7 in); length 19.00m (62 ft 4 in); height 5.20m (17 ft 0.7 in); wing span 40.00m² (430.57 sq ft)
Weights: empty 12,000kg (26,455 lb); loaded 19,000kg (41,888 lb)
Performance: maximum speed 2,500km/h (1,553 mph); service ceiling 18,000m (59,055 ft); range 1,850km (1,150 miles)
Armament: two 30mm cannon plus provision for disposable stores up to an unstated weight

A Shenyang J-8 statically displayed at the 1987 Paris International Airshow.

Singapore Aircraft Industries A-4 Super Skyhawk

First flown in June 1954 as a carrierborne lightweight attack airplane, the Skyhawk is still in service in its original form but has also been developed as a potent land-based attacker. The type is undergoing something of a renaissance in South-East Asia in variants rebuilt with modern electronics and, in the Super Skyhawk variant, turbofan power for 35% greater rate of climb, 40% better acceleration and 15% higher maximum speed.

Countries of Origin: U.S.A. and Singapore
Type: light ground-attack fighter
Crew: One
Power Plant: one General Electric F404-GE-100D non-afterburning turbofan, rated at 48.06kN (10,800 lb) thrust
Dimensions: span 8.38m (27 ft 6 in); length 12.29m (40 ft 4 in); height 4.57m (15 ft 10 in); wing area 24.16m² (260.00 sq ft)
Weights: empty not available; loaded about 12,437kg (27,420 lb)
Performance: maximum speed 1,100km/h (684 mph); service ceiling not available; range not available
Armament: two 30mm cannon plus provision for up to 4,153kg (9,155 lb) of disposable stores

An SAI Super Skyhawk on display at Asian Aerospace 88.

Sukhoi Su-7BMK 'Fitter-A'

Despite its dismally low range on internal fuel, which means that the type has to carry drop tanks rather than bombs on any but the very shortest missions, the Su-7 remains a classic ground-attack fighter. The type first flew in 1955, and after development in four combat and three trainer versions was then transformed in 1966 by the adoption of variable-geometry outer wing panels. This swing-wing series is still in production after development through Su-17, Su-20 and Su-22 forms.

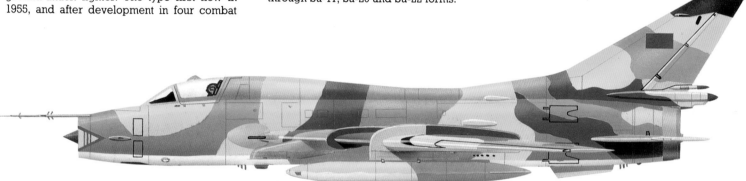

Country of Origin: U.S.S.R.
Type: ground attack fighter
Crew: one
Power Plant: one Lyul'ka AL-74-1 afterburning turbojet, rated at 98.10kN (22,046 lb) thrust
Dimensions: span 8.93m (29 ft 3.5 in); length 17.37m (57 ft 0 in); height 4.57m (15 ft 0 in); wing area 31.50m² (339.10 sq ft)
Weights: empty 8,620kg (19,004 lb); loaded 13,500kg (29,762 lb)
Performance: maximum speed 1,700km/h (1,055 mph); service ceiling 15,150m (49,700 ft); range 345km (215 miles) radius on a lo-lo-lo mission
Armament: two 30mm cannon plus provision for up to 2,500kg (5,511 lb) of disposable stores

Sukhoi 'Fitter-As' of the Polish Air Force.

Sukhoi Su-24 'Fencer-C'

When it entered service in 1974 this was the Soviets' first true variable-geometry airplane, and is an extremely capable type that has been developed through several major marks from the initial 'Fencer-A' long-range interdictor. These are the higher-weight 'Fencer-B', the electronically updated 'Fencer-C' with more powerful engines, the 'Fencer-D' with an inflight-refuelling probe and new nose radar, the 'Fencer-E' electronic warfare model, and the 'Fencer-F' reconnaissance platform.

Country of Origin: U.S.S.R.
Type: all-weather strike, ground attack and interdiction aircraft
Crew: two
Power Plant: two Lyul'ka AL-21F-3 afterburning turbojets, rated at 109.87kN (24,691 lb) thrust each
Dimensions: span 17.50m (57 ft 5 in) spread and 10.50m (34 ft 5.5 in) swept; length 21.29m (69 ft 10 in); height 6.00m (19 ft 8 in); wing area 47.00m² (505.92 sq ft) spread and 42.50m² (457.48 sq ft) swept
Weights: empty 19,000 kg (41,887 lb); loaded 41,000kg (90,388 lb)
Performance: maximum speed 2,320km/h (1,441 mph); service ceiling 16,500m (54,135 ft); range 1,300km (805 miles) radius on a hi-lo-hi mission with a 3,000kg (6,614 lb) warload
Armament: one 30mm six-barrel cannon plus provision for 11,000kg (24,250 lb) of disposable stores

A Sukhoi Su-24 'Fencer-D', seen here at the Soviet Union's Toshino Air Show in 1989.

Sukhoi Su-27 'Flanker-B'

This air-superiority fighter is the Soviet counterpart to the Americans' McDonnell Douglas F-15, and began to enter service in 1986 as an advanced type with blended aerodynamics, relaxed stability and a fly-by-wire control system plus advanced sensors that include modern radar, an infra-red search and track system, a laser ranger and a helmet-mounted sight system. The 'Flanker-A' was probably the pre-production variant, the current 'Flanker-B' being complemented by the 'Flanker-C' two-seater with full combat capability.

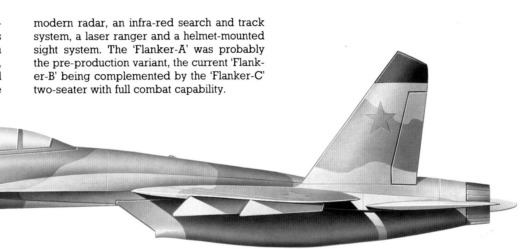

Country of Origin: U.S.S.R.
Type: air-superiority fighter with secondary ground attack capability
Crew: one
Power Plant: two Lyul'ka AL-31F afterburning turbofans, rated at 133.42kN (29,982 lb) thrust each
Dimensions: span 14.70m (48 ft 2.75 in); length 21.90m (71ft 10.2 in); height 5.50m (18 ft 0.5 in); wing area 46.50m² (500.54 sq ft)
Weights: empty 17,700kg (39,012 lb); loaded 30,000kg (66,138 lb)
Performance: maximum speed 2,495km/h (1,550 mph); service ceiling 15,000+m (49,215+ ft); range 1,500km (932 miles) radius on a hi-hi-hi mission
Armament: one 30mm cannon plus provision for up to 6,000kg (13,228 lb) of disposable stores

The Su-27 'Flanker-B'. The Sukhoi design bureau is currently designing a naval version.

Yakovlev Yak-38 'Forger-A'

Developed from the Yak-36 experimental prototype for carrierborne service from 1976, the Yak-38 is a STOVL type using a combination of one vectored-thrust and two direct-lift turbojets. The type has only modest operational capability, yet is providing the Soviet naval air arm with experience in operating fixed-wing airplanes pending the delivery of true aircraft-carriers. The single-seat 'Forger-A' is complemented by the two-seat 'Forger-B' trainer.

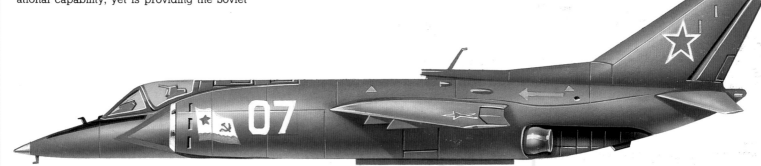

Country of Origin: U.S.S.R.
Type: carrierborne multi-role STOVL combat aircraft
Crew: one
Power Plant: one Lyul'ka AL-21F vectored-thrust non-afterburning turbojet, rated at 80kN (17,989 lb) thrust, and two Koliesov ZM non-afterburning lift turbojets, rated at 35kN (7,870 lb) thrust each
Dimensions: span 7.32m (24 ft 0.2 in); length 15.50m (50 ft 10.3 in); height 4.37 (14 ft 4 in); wing area 18.50m² (199.14 sq ft)
Weights: empty 7,385kg (16,281 lb); loaded 13,000kg (28,660 lb)
Performance: maximum speed 1,110km/h (627 mph); service ceiling 12,000m (39,370 ft); range 240km (150 miles) radius on a lo-lo-lo mission with maximum warload
Armament: provision for up to 3,600kg (7,937 lb) of disposable stores

Three Yak-38 parked aboard a 'Kiev' class Soviet aircraft carrier, with folded wingtips to save deck space and open lift engine intakes.